Natural Medicine

by

Mawlana Shaykh Nazim al-Haqqani

Foreword by
Shaykh Hisham Kabbani

Institute for Spirituality & Cultural Advancement

Natural Medicine

Published by:

Institute for Spirituality & Cultural Advancement (ISCA)
17195 Silver Parkway #201
Fenton, MI 48430
United States
phone: (810)-744-4489
email: staff@sufilive.com

Author Mawlana Shaykh Nazim Adil al-Haqqani.

Ayat ash-Shifa: Quranic Verses of Healing

In the Name of Allah the Most Merciful, the Beneficent

﴾ وَيَشْفِ صُدُورَ قَوْمٍ مُّؤْمِنِينَ ﴿

And [God] shall heal the breast of the believers. (Surat at-Tawba, 9:14)

﴾ يَا أَيُّهَا النَّاسُ قَدْ جَاءتْكُم مَّوْعِظَةٌ مِّن رَّبِّكُمْ وَشِفَاء لِّمَا فِي الصُّدُورِ وَهُدًى وَرَحْمَةٌ لِّلْمُؤْمِنِينَ ﴿

Mankind there has come to you a guidance from your Lord and a healing for (the diseases) in your hearts, and for those who believe a guidance and a mercy. (Surah Yunus, 10:57)

﴾ يخْرُجُ مِن بُطُونِهَا شَرَابٌ مُّخْتَلِفٌ أَلْوَانُهُ فِيهِ شِفَاء لِلنَّاسِ ﴿

There issues from within the bodies of the bee a drink of varying colors wherein is healing for mankind. (Surat an-Nahl, 16:69)

﴾ وَنُنَزِّلُ مِنَ الْقُرْآنِ مَا هُوَ شِفَاء وَرَحْمَةٌ لِّلْمُؤْمِنِينَ ﴿

And We sent down in the Quran such things that have healing and mercy for the believers (Surat an-Najm, 17:82)

﴾ وَإِذَا مَرِضْتُ فَهُوَ يَشْفِينِ ﴿

And when I am ill, it is [God] who cures me." (Surat ash-Shu`ara, 26:80)

﴾ قُلْ هُوَ لِلَّذِينَ آمَنُوا هُدًى وَشِفَاء ﴿

And declare (O Muhammad) that [the Quran] is a guidance and healing for the believers. (Surah Fussilat, 41:44)

Contents

Ayat ash-Shifa: Quranic Verses of Healing iv

Foreword: Prophetic Medicine - Cure for All Ills 1

Introduction 5

ANAEMIA: 13

ANGINA: 13

APPENDICITIS: 13

ARTHRITIS: 13

ASTHMA: 13

BEDWETTING: 14

BEE-STING: 14

BLADDER+ KIDNEY INFECTION: 14

BLOOD-TRANSFUSION: 14

BLOOD-LOSS: 14

BRAIN-CONCUSSION: 14

BURN: 15

CAESARIAN: 15

CANCER: 16

CANCER IN THE THYROID GLAND: 16

CHILDREN WHO DON'T GROW: 16

CHOLERA: 16

CHOLESTROL: 17

COMPULSIVE-WASHING: 17

CONSTIPATION: 17

COUGH / BRONCHITIS: 17

CROSS-EYEDNESS:...18

DEAFNESS DUE TO DIRT IN THE EARS:.............................18

DEPRESSION:...18

DIABETES:..18

DIARRHOEA:..18

DRUG ABUSE:...18

EAR-ACHE:...19

EPILEPSY:...19

FARSIGHTEDNESS:...19

FEAR:..20

FIRST AID:..20

GALLSTONES:..20

GIVING WIND:...20

HAIR-LOSS:..20

HAY-FEVER:...20

HEAD-ACHE:..21

PREVENTING A HEART-ATTACK:..21

HEART PROBLEMS IN GENERAL:.......................................21

HEART-BURN:..21

HEMORRHOIDS:...22

HERPES:...22

HIGH BLOOD PRESSURE:..22

WEAK IMMUNE SYSTEM:..22

INSOMNIA:..22

ISCHIATITIS:..22

KIDNEY-STONES:..23

LIVER+GALL STONES: 23

LOW BLOOD PRESSURE: 23

MALARIA: 23

MASSAGE: 23

MEASLES: 24

MENISCUS: 24

MORBUS CHRON/CHOLITIS ULCEROSA CHRON: 24

MOUTH INFECTION VIRUS: 24

MUSCULAR DYSTROPHY: 24

MUMPS: 25

NAIL-BITING: 25

NEURODERMITIS: 25

NOSE-BLEEDING: 25

OVERWEIGHT: 25

PARALYSIS: 25

PARODONTOSE: 26

PELVIS-PAIN: 26

PIMPLES: 26

PREGNANCY & ULTRASOUND: 26

PSORIASIS: 27

RHEUMATISM: 27

RUNNING NOSE: 27

SHOCK: 27

SCHIZOPHRENICS: 27

SCORPION-BITE: 28

SEA-SICKNESS: 28

SHORT-SIGHTEDNESS: 28

SKIN-CANCER: 28

SMOKER'S LEG: 28

SNAKE-BITE: 29

SORE THROAT/BEGINNING OF A COLD: 29

SPRAINED ANKLE: 29

STAMMERING: 29

STERILITY/INFERTILITY: 29

STOMACH PAIN: 29

SUNSTROKE: 30

GNASHING AND BITING OF TEETH: 30

TORN MUSCLE: 30

STIFFNESS OF FINGERS WHEN WAKING UP: 30

VARICOSE VEINS: 30

VAGINAL PARASITE: 30

WATER IN THE LEGS: 31

WARTS: 31

WEAK MEMORY: 31

YELLOW FEVER: 31

GLOSSARY: 33

Foreword

Prophetic Medicine - Cure for All Ills

Allah made for every sickness a remedy. We must not accept that there is any sickness without a remedy. The Prophet Muhammad, peace be upon him, mentioned that for every sickness there is a cure. This is the Prophet to whom Allah gave the power of Isra'a and M'iraj, the Night Journey from Mecca to Jerusalem and then the Heavenly Ascension to the Divine Presence, to reach the Divine Presence of Allah Almighty. It was a miraculous event and many did not believe it until the Prophet, peace be upon him, gave them proof, telling them what he had seen on the road to Masjid al-Aqsa in Jerusalem. He told them about the caravans that were due to arrive in Mecca, and they then immediately believed him as no one would know such detail except one who had been there and seen them.

The Prophet was sent by Allah as a mercy, a *rahma*, to humanity. Every mercy therefore falls under the mercy of the Prophet ﷺ: health is a mercy, wealth is a mercy, to be in a good position in this life is a mercy, to be in good standing in the Hereafter is a mercy, every shower of rain (*rahma* in Arabic) or snow is mercy. All of this mercy that is coming, Allah put in the heart of our master Muhammad and the hearts of his family members, upon all of them be peace, because his family is his blood and his blood is holy. So the one on whom Allah bestowed His Mercy knows what kind of remedy will help against every sickness.

I witnessed many illnesses cured by the remedies prescribed by both my grandshaykh Abdallah al-Fa'iz al-Daghestani and Mawlana Shaykh Nazim al-Haqqani. These cures come from the Prophet ﷺ: it is Prophetic Medicine (*at-Tibb an-Nabawi*) that so many people are using today regardless of name, sometimes coming under the name "alternative medicine," "Yunani medicine," "traditional medicine" or others.

Real seclusion bears fruit. A real seclusion is not one that you demand from your shaykh, but one that is demanded of you: where the shaykh

1

calls you out of the blue and says, "You! Go to seclusion." When you are in such a seclusion and get trained very well, becoming more experienced, every sickness comes to you on its own and says, "I am this type of sickness and the remedy for me is this." According to the level of the one performing seclusion, there will be prescriptions coming from heavenly sources for many difficult medical situations.

One of the worst sicknesses that people are facing today is cancer. I heard, witnessed, and saw from my shaykh that cancer can be cured and eliminated from a patient, but the patient must accept what they are required to do for the cure. My sister was a medical doctor, and she became ill with cancer. As a doctor she wasn't able to accept anything other than what she had studied. She went to Shaykh Nazim in the late 1980's to speak with him about her case. He told her not to operate. As a doctor however, she insisted on it–she did the operation on her breast and lived 15 years before passing away.

My auntie, who was in her early 50's, also had a cancer. She went to Shaykh Nazim and Grandshaykh Abdallah for advice. Her doctors had already decided that she needed to have an operation. The night before the operation was to occur, we went to Grandshaykh's house. This was in the 1970's. He told us to take her out of the hospital, that if she didn't do the operation she would have another 30 years of life. That night we went back to Beirut and removed her from the hospital. The next morning they were searching for her, not knowing what had happened! She ended up living another 30 years, passing away at age 85. Meanwhile, my sister who went through with her operation ended up living only another 15 years.

Shaykh Nazim is carrying knowledge of Prophetic Medicine, *at-Tibb an-Nabawi*, that he has inherited by his spiritual connection with the Prophet, peace be upon him, through the Naqshbandi Golden Chain of saints. He explained that there is a dormant cancer in every human being. It doesn't awaken except in certain patients. If we touch the cancer however, it will go crazy. Instead of growing slowly, if we touch it with a knife the cancer will go wild and spread. He said the best thing in that case is to take onion juice. The Prophet ﷺ said that although onion and garlic have a bad smell, they are cures for 70 different illnesses that cannot be cured by any other means. So the People of Allah recommend onion juice.

Just recently, I was in New York. One of the students brought a lady to me, saying that this was the lady who had cancer before and thanks be to Allah, she'd been cured. A year before I had been in New York, and they had brought her to me saying that she had a tumor in her head. She had one child. I told her to drink onion juice. I also read Surat al-Fatiha (the opening chapter of the Quran) seven times upon some water on behalf of Shaykh Nazim, and told her to drink it. One week later she had an X-ray at the hospital and the tumor was gone. It's not because I read or she took the onion juice, it's because she believed that it could happen. She believed in Allah and she believed in the Prophet, peace be upon him. So a year later I saw her again, and she had been cancer-free for the whole time with no operation and no chemotherapy.

My recommendation for people with this problem is to take onion juice and to read Surat al-Fatiha seven times on water, or coffee for example, and drink it. They could alternatively read Surat al-Fatiha seven times and blow on themselves. If they are not able, someone else can read Surat al-Fatiha for them.

May Allah give us healing, *shifa*, and give those who are suffering from this sickness healing also. May Allah make it easy on everyone. He is The Healer (al-Shafi).

Ya Rabbi (Oh my Lord), You are the One that cures, there is no one else, we are coming to You, requesting through our master Muhammad and through Your saints. We are weak and sinful servants, but we are coming to you. Where else is there to go? Your Door is the one people can come to. We are coming to Your door asking You to cure every human being, especially those sufferers who have children- to give them happiness in their lives. And to cure us also, and our children and to extend our lives to see our master the Mahdi and our master Jesus, upon them both be Allah's peace, for that will be the best time - the Golden

Era. We are asking that Allah will accept from all of us, for the sake of the children here as their supplication is accepted. For the sake of the saints, our master Muhammad, and Ahl al-Bayt (the Family of the Prophet, peace be upon them all) may Allah accept from us *bi hurmati 'l-habib bi hurmati 'l*-Fatihah, and by the sanctity of the Beloved, by the sanctity of the Opening Chapter of the Quran.

Shaykh Hisham Kabbani
Fenton, Michigan
January 2008/1429

Introduction

This is a short introduction for a new medicine and treatment booklet. People in our days are very much in need of this, because illnesses are increasing and it is becoming more and more impossible for physicians or scientists to find names, treatments or medicines to cure these illnesses.

Simple illnesses have simple medicines, but during the development of mankind and the growing up of disobedience, the illnesses also started to be disobedient against the medicines and could not be cured anymore. By permission of Allah Almighty a very grave illness can also be defeated by simple medicine but the more mankind became disloyal and disobedient to Divine Laws, the more illnesses were impossible to cure, even the most simple ones.

Nowadays you must use so many medicines for curing. Don't believe that those medicines and operations are of any use! If people were obedient servants, Allah Almighty could be able to give health and to take away that illness. As long as people think that medicines will take away illness, the illnesses will never go away.

The heavy pressure of artificial medicines will make them sleepy or even to lose their consciousness. Then when the powerful medicine and poison is taken away, the bacteria and microbes awake and begin to rush and to eat the organs because Allah Almighty gives the command: "Destroy!"

The reason for all of this is disobedience. These people never think that health comes from Allah, they think that health is a result of tablets, pills and operations. That is a big sin.

Once I visited a doctor in Karachi, Pakistan. It was a simple clinic. Over the door was written a Holy Verse from the Holy Quran: "*If I will be ill, my Lord will give me health.*" (26:80).

That is a big warning and attention for everyone coming to a doctor. It is not correct to say: "This doctor doesn't know anything." The cure doesn't come from the doctor and from medicines, but from Allah. When people left this belief and left Paradise, thousands and thousands of illnesses fell over them, even though there are only 360 organs.

Some people come to me after having gone to so many doctors. They say, "No-one knows how to cure this illness!" What I understand is that every day new illnesses occur which not even professors know anything about. Partly very strange illnesses concerning: eyes, ears, tongue, brain, throat, heart, liver, lungs, stomach, kidney, bones, blood, nose. In our days such a complexity comes out of our bodies. People get ill, feel ill, go to a physician, to laboratories, make x- rays, feel ill, go again and after having made a full check-up the doctors tell them:

'There is nothing wrong.'

'But I am ill!'

'Everything is alright.'

'I feel ill'.

That is another kind of punishment, to feel ill. There is no medicine, but they will get drugs to forget; to make some parts of the brain not to function. The physician will feel obliged to give drugs and so, even though the patient is not ill, the doctor will poison him. Millions have this kind of illness.

The last thing will be that the doctors say "We must cut open your head." Then they touch the brain. This is the most difficult operation, no one should accept it. With heart operations it is the same: it is dangerous and hopeless.

To use a knife is always harmful, but nowadays physicians mostly hurry up and cut. That is so difficult and so harmful. Without using a knife, there is a treatment for every illness, a natural medicine. It may take more time, but it has no side effects.

We believe that there are many reasons for people to get ill. Some are physical reasons, some spiritual. And so, as believers, we do not accept that every illness only comes from a disease and only has something to do with this life. It is also a heavenly reaction that affects people and makes them ill.

All prophets advised their nations, their believers, their followers, to use charity as a protection against illnesses. It is not only in Islam that we say that charity gives you a shelter against illnesses. Every religion has declared through their prophets the importance of giving or doing charity.

That is the reason that we are repeating the same orders like all the prophets were giving, including the last prophet, peace be upon him, and upon them all. Charities must be done or given first. Before using any medicine, people must try to cure themselves by doing charity. That is why charity is so important.

When we understand this, treatment is easy for believers. For unbelievers the cure is very difficult. The souls help the believers to be cured, but unbelievers have souls that are against themselves and these will never support them. So the cure of unbelievers will take longer and longer or may be even stay until the last moment of their lives. Believers, however, because their souls support and help them, can quickly be treated and cured.

So the most important factor for the treatment and the cure of an illness is to give charity, "sadaqa."

It is the most terrible and most dangerous time for living people and for them to be safe against all unknown illnesses. As long as physicians and researchers are searching they will find more illnesses and more medicines and treatments against them. It will be impossible to make a limit. The number of illnesses and the number of treatments existing in our days have reached a climax. This makes physicians and scientists tired and they are coming to a point of becoming hopeless to be able to prevent the spreading of illnesses or to be able to control them.

Therefore we are looking for some main medicine to treat mankind. First treatment of all for every ill person is: they must believe.

Unbelief brings endless reasons of illnesses as a punishment. And so, as a first treatment for all mankind: It is the most important thing to believe in the existence of the Lord of the Universes.

Secondly, mankind needs to accept advice: first of all from the Lord of Heavens, secondly from His Prophets and thirdly from the Friends of the Lord. If they are not hearing and listening to the Heavenly Advices of the Lord Almighty Allah, of His beloved Prophet Sayyidina Mohammed, peace be upon him, of all prophets and also not accepting advice from the other inheritors of prophets: the holy ones, the Friends of Allah, they will suffer and there will be no more cure for them.

Perhaps the treatment will even be a punishment for them. In our days nearly every treatment is through surgery and surgery is not a real treatment. It was not until this century that surgery started to be used in this exaggerated way.

Today surgery is the most important treatment for illnesses. Perhaps 99% of the physicians want to use the knife of surgery and nothing else. They want to cut, to sew, to add, to destroy and nothing else! That is not treatment, it is a punishment.

That is why we are saying: everyone must believe in the existence of the Lord of Heavens, must believe in the existence of the Creator of the whole universe and must believe in His Will Power. They must also believe that the treatment of His servants only can come from His Will. Only if He is willing, can treatment come to ill people. If He does not want, only more punishment will come, not treatment.

For this reason only a small percentage of the people have not had a knife cutting their body. That is one way in which this punishment reaches the whole world from East to West.

Illness is a punishment for people living in our days. After getting that punishment, the treatment, which they are asking for is the next punishment, and the result of it is that they will be crippled. In our days every part of the body has been cut and opened and has suffered: head, heart, liver. Every part of the body has been touched by knives. All this is another punishment; it will not give the patient rest, never! It is not a treatment.

With my given authority I am advising all mankind to hear and to listen to the words of the Lord. If they are not listening and obeying, that punishment will just rain on them every day and there will be no treatment and no medicine for them. There will be no happiness and no rest for their bodies or minds or for their hearts.

This includes to listen to His beloved Messenger Sayyidina Mohammed, peace be upon him. Allah Almighty taught him every kind of treatment. Every illness is well known by the Seal of Prophets and he has been given heavenly knowledges concerning medicines and treatments for every kind of illness.

We are advising to use some of these divine treatments, just simple medicines, natural medicines, because our bodies belong to nature and the body's cure can only come through natural medicines. Every artificial thing that grows in our days is against the nature of mankind. Therefore it must be stopped! Every artificial, synthetic medicine is against the nature of our structure and so it must be stopped. It harms and damages the structure of our bodies.

People of the 20th century have lost their patience. Mankind has no more patience. They are asking for quick treatment, and treatment through natural medicine takes time, but mankind has no patience and ask for their pain and suffering to stop quickly. Therefore they want new artificial strong medicines and it is not important for them if they are damaging their bodies. Their only interest is to stop their pain and suffering quickly.

An important advice for ill people: to be patient enough to use natural medicines. These natural medicines have been used through centuries since the beginning of life on earth. Mostly they have been taught to the people through heavenly knowledges, through prophets and messengers. It has been completed by the Seal of Prophets, Sayyidina Mohammed ﷺ.

Mankind must also try to keep their bodies safe. The way of doing this, is to keep everything away which harms our body. Everything which harms our physical body is mentioned in the heavenly messages, heavenly knowledges, heavenly advices and heavenly treatments. You must keep these rules and stay away from every damaging and harming thing which is written in the Holy Books and is prohibited by the Lord Almighty Allah. As long as you are going against these, you will be punished and have no treatment.

Illnesses never come without a reason: either it is as a punishment to make that person to obey, or it is to demonstrate the treatment for others.

And so, who drinks alcohol must be punished. All drinks that harm the body are prohibited and should not be drunk. Anyone who comes against this and says, "Oh, just a little bit" will be punished just a little bit. If a person drinks a little bit of poison he will suffer a little bit. If he takes more, he will suffer more. This is because prohibited things are poison, spiritually and physically.

If anyone smokes, he must be punished. If only a little bit, he must be punished a little bit. If very much, the punishment will be very big.

If a person eats pork and that which is prohibited of dead animals, it will harm his body and he must be punished.

If man and woman make illegal actions: once, twice, three times, something may attack her and him and they will be punished. Until people leave all these things that I am mentioning, they will be punished sooner or later.

In the time of Prophet, peace be upon him, most of the people were ignorant and they were doing everything. Then Islam came, they accepted it and were cleaned by following the Lord's command. And so, if anyone today is doing wrong out of ignorance and then says, "I am finishing this and now, my Lord, I am listening and obeying", then the illnesses can be carried away by Divine Will without even using any medicine. That is the treatment for him or for her then, and it is alright.

When unbelief, "*Kufr*", is taken away, everything else that is bad is taken away too.

But it must be well known that every prohibited thing brings illnesses, unknown illnesses. As in our days unknown illnesses are coming to us through homosexual people, and there is no medicine, no treatment, because it is against the Holy Command of the Lord of Heavens. If they find some cure, another hopeless illness will come, because the Creator creates so many bacteria and viruses. It is endless.

Therefore the first protection is not to put the body in front of danger. In the same way as someone who puts their hand on an electric wire also will feel the painful reaction.

As for children born with illnesses, it is not they but their parents who are the ones being punished, not the children. If people take care, then they are protected. For these people it is easy to be treated. Simple! Even water, the source of life, gives them treatment and can be medicine.

Allah created cold water and hot water. You may lie in cold water or in hot water or in mud and your body can be as if renewed. You may drink some water and it can clean your insides. You may eat grapes and it will be like medicine. You may eat melon and it will give you strength. You may eat wheat and it will give you power. Everything that we are using as a grace or as a favour from Allah Almighty will at the same time be power and medicine for us. In that way, there is no need to look for other medicines because the Lord of Heavens, the Lord of the Children of Adam, created everything and gave a treatment for everything. Life power is in every food and likewise every food is a medicine. The only condition is to say, "In the name of Allah Who created this for His servants' wealth and health" when eating or drinking. Use everything in His Name and it will be medicine and treatment for you.

That is the only purpose for which the Lord created it. Not to be avoided by His servants. When you are going to important physicians or specialists who then say, "Don't eat this, don't touch that, don't use that!" That is not a treatment, it is a punishment because you were not using it in the name of the Lord that created it. And so Allah prevents you and as a punishment the doctors will tell you: "Don't eat sugar, don't eat fruits, don't eat meat, don't touch butter, and don't touch honey!"

Mankind must learn to come and declare their humbleness towards the Lord of Heavens. As long as they are not doing that, as long as they are not declaring their servant hood, they will be punished and nothing will give them any treatment or health, even if they fill the whole world with medicines. The whole world can be filled with doctors and medicines and specialists and still it will be impossible to give mankind any health or rest or peace or satisfaction or take away their suffering and miseries. This must be well-known.

I am speaking to all mankind so that they may be warned by Heavenly Warnings. Everything that has been declared in this small booklet has been said with this condition. I hope for endless blessings by the Lord of Heavens for it to be useful for mankind. May Allah bless us and accept our excuse and grant us from His endless blessings so that we may believe and be good servants.

For the successful use of the medicines in this book there are three conditions:

1. The acceptance of one Creator
2. No drinking of alcohol
3. No smoking of tobacco

From Allah is all success.

Shaykh Nazim al-Haqqani
Lefke, Cyprus
1989

ANAEMIA:

Eat carrots cooked with raisins and sugar. Every morning and evening for 40 days.

ANGINA:

Rub vinegar on neck and head in the morning and in the evening. Keep warm: wear woolen socks and woolen cap.

APPENDICITIS:

Grind barley and boil with milk. Put it on the appendix area of the body once or twice while still hot. Leave it there the whole day and the whole night.

Drink milk boiled with 5 cloves (ground) and mixed with honey, while still hot. Morning, noon and evening one cup.

ARTHRITIS:

Boil sheet-trotters with plenty of water until it turns to jelly.

Take some spoonfuls every morning before eating or drinking anything else. Repeat 40 days.

ASTHMA:

Take a handful of linseeds, grind them and boil with a Turkish tea glass filled with milk.

Put the mixture on a cloth and cover in front from neck to belly and in the back from neck to waist. Cover with wool and keep overnight.

Repeat 3, 5 or 7 nights.

And/or

Take a radish, mash it and mix one spoonful of it with one spoon of honey. Repeat once in the morning and once in the evening for 15 days.

BEDWETTING:

Take a big spoon of soapwort (*Saponaria officinalis*) mixed with sugar before going to bed.

BEE-STING:

Put vinegar with a piece of cotton wool on the sting.

BLADDER+ KIDNEY INFECTION:

Take 5 kilos of cucumber. Peel it. Take the skin and put it with 3 bunches of parsley into a pot with twice as much water. Let it boil. When half of the water is boiled off, sieve it and put the juice into the fridge. Drink one Turkish teaglass-full every morning, noon and evening until the infection is gone.

BLOOD-TRANSFUSION:

Instead of doing a blood-transfusion clean your blood by drinking a soup of: bones-marrow with black pepper, ginger, cinnamon and cloves.

BLOOD-LOSS:

Patience! Your body produces new blood by itself. Within 40 days the lost blood will be reproduced.

Drink the same soup as in 'Blood-transfusion' and also sheep milk with honey.

BRAIN-CONCUSSION:

Don't move and don't touch it! Pay *sadaqa*.

Eat 21 raisins with seeds every morning.

Every morning, noon and evening drink milk with honey, cold or warm. Never allow to have an operation done.

BURN:

Put cold water and then olive-oil on the burn.

CAESARIAN:

I don't believe that there are babies that don't come out. The only problem is that we are impatient. The One Who has planted the fetus in the womb of the mother must also bring it out. But we are not patient people.

Another reason for caesarians to be done a lot is that people prefer for a caesarian than for a normal birth. I don't believe that the doctors are doing it for the best of the mothers. I don't believe that they are doing a good and a right thing.

Even last week I was saying, concerning my daughter-in-law, "Don't do it, let her bring the baby!" Their gynecologist said, "Everything is normal. But it is the first baby, so may be the labor pains will last until tonight. Go to your home to rest and come back in the afternoon!" The mistake was, that Istanbul is too big a city to go and come like that, so in the afternoon when the pain increased, she had to be taken to another hospital that was nearer. In the private ward two other gynecologists had a look at her and said, "Oh, this is too much pain for her, her hands are already blue, which means it is dangerous. And the baby is upside down. The feet are at the bottom. What can we do?"

The doctor-in-charge answered, "If it is the wrong way around, you must do a caesarian." And even though my daughter- in-law shouted that she didn't want that, they did it.

The first doctor that she had visited in the morning, said afterwards to me that everything had been alright and normal. Also that the head was lying like it should, not like the other doctors had said. This doctor who confirmed that everything had been normal all along was the one who had been examining her all the months of pregnancy, so he should know.

So I don't believe doctors when it comes to deciding when to make a caesarian. They take money and cut. And their patients, who don't know what is going on, how are they to decide whether it is dangerous for the mother, or not? I don't accept it.

CANCER:

Crush onion and drink Turkish tea-glass full of its juice every morning and evening in the morning before eating or drinking anything else.

Repeat for 40 days.

CANCER IN THE THYROID GLAND:

Repeat for 40 days:

Every morning before eating or drinking anything else: drink a glass (Turkish tea-glass) full of the squeezed juice of an onion.

CHILDREN WHO DON'T GROW:

Pay *sadaqa*!

Give them marrow soup to eat and sheep milk to drink.

CHOLERA:

Don't eat or drink anything!

Take Epsom salts to clean yourself inside.

Then drink a small cup of kerosene in the morning. No food during one day and if possible also no drinking. If necessary, then drink the water of cooked unwashed rice.

CHOLESTROL:

The main reason for cholesterol is drinking wine. Wine collects the cholesterol in the blood like a magnet pulls iron together.

Eat with every meal a salad with onion and vinegar.

COMPULSIVE-WASHING:

A full body wash is enough 2 times a day. If more than that, then:

Put your arms up to your elbows into a dustbin. Then cover face and head with the dirt of the dustbin. Leave it on the body for 10 minutes, then wash.

CONSTIPATION:

Boil 3-5 figs in water.

Drink the water and eat the figs before going to sleep.

COUGH / BRONCHITIS:

Before going to sleep at night:

- heat 3 tablespoons of olive-oil
- drench a big piece of cotton-wool with the hot olive-oil wrap it up in newspaper
- put it on the chest while still hot
- cover with a woolen sweater and leave until morning.

Repeat 10 nights.

Also drink one cup four times a day of water and honey boiled with:

Cloves Cinnamon black pepper ginger

or / and

Boil one big spoon of corn flour with a cup of milk. Add sugar or honey and drink hot before sleeping. Cover your head preferably with wool.

CROSS-EYEDNESS:

Crush 3 cloves of garlic and mix with a spoon of honey. Eat every morning before eating or drinking anything else. Repeat for 40 days.

If not gone, repeat for another 40 days.

DEAFNESS DUE TO DIRT IN THE EARS:

Put hot olive-oil in a syringe and put 3 drops into each ear. After 2 minutes clean with cotton wool.

DEPRESSION:

Visit hospitals, mental-houses and prisons regularly and your own depression will run away quickly.

DIABETES:

Drink tea made out of goose-grass (*gallium aparine*) several times a day.

DIARRHOEA:

Take one big spoon of finely ground coffee and mix it with lemon-juice. Once swallowed may be followed by a glass of water.

No drinking or eating for several hours.

DRUG ABUSE:

(like alcohol, tobacco, heroin, cocaine)

Condition is that the drug-abuser wants to stop and uses will-power to do so.

Take a bottle of water. Pray the first surah of the Holy Quran: Fatiha 40 times. After each Fatiha blow into the bottle of water.

Every time when you feel an urge to use a drug, take a sip of the water instead.

EAR-ACHE:

Take a small spoon of black seeds (*Nigella Sativa*) and fry them and smash them. Then add olive oil, heat it and put 7 drops with a syringe into the ear every morning and evening until better.

EPILEPSY:

There are 2 main groups of epileptics:

- Possessed by jinns.
- Dysfunction of the brain.

If the attack is caused by jinns, it is useful to put a piece of iron on the back of the neck until the attack is over. Any iron may do: knife, spoon, etc.

They should always wear a *tawiz* covered in leather.

Any *surah* (verse from the Holy Quran) may be recited on them.

This illness is sometimes caused by babies falling on their heads and it then can happen that they bleed in the head and this blood clotted and damages the rest of the brain.

These patients should be shaved on top of their head and cupped. Only the clotted blood should be taken, not the clean. Repeat 3 times. Then take cow-gall on a feather and put it on the same place. Mix butter and black seeds (*nigella sativa*), thick and put on top. Tie the head for 3 days changing the head-band every 24 hours and putting new mixture on it. One treatment enough, *insha Allah*.

FARSIGHTEDNESS:

Crush 1 big or 3 small cloves of garlic and mix with honey (one teaspoon) and eat every morning before eating or drinking anything else.

Pay *sadaqa* 40 days.

FEAR:

This belongs to your spiritual life

If you are a non-believer you must start to believe, because no-one will give you peace except Allah.

If you are a believer you have no reason to fear if you never harmed anybody. If you did, or if you did a disliked action, you must stop it because the harm will come back as a boomerang to you. If you insist on being rebellious, your fear will stay.

FIRST AID:

Tie the wounds so as to avoid blood-loss. Keep warm.

Give fresh lemon juice or *ayran* (sour milk) to drink.

GALLSTONES:

Drink a Turkish coffee-cup full of radish juice every evening and morning. Continue treatment for 15 - 40 days.

GIVING WIND:

Drink tea of aniseed every morning, noon and evening.

HAIR-LOSS:

When washing your hair don't use other shampoos, only olive-oil soap or laurel soap.

After wash rub scalp with olive-oil.

For women: when in public try to cover head to avoid evil-eye.

HAY-FEVER:

Every morning and evening:

Put 3 drops of olive-oil into each nostril, Cover your head at all times!

HEAD-ACHE:

There are so many reasons for headaches. It is important to find out why. Sometimes another illness in the body causes it. If that is not the case, then the reason is the nervous system in the neck hurting.

Massage head and neck, put a piece of material drenched in vinegar around your head. Cover your head.

Boil 15 big brown beans, drink the water and eat the beans.

PREVENTING A HEART-ATTACK:

A heart-attack is also a punishment for using our bodies without taking any care. The most harmful thing for the veins is smoking. Your veins never forgive you for smoking, so:

Stop smoking.

Eat as much quinces as possible: marmalade, salad, tea of the buds (prepared in any you like). Don't worry!

HEART PROBLEMS IN GENERAL:

Put a medium sized onion in a tin filled with hot ashes and heat on fire until the onion is roasted. Eat first thing in the morning.

40 days.

Also a healing method for cleaning up the body after many years of smoking.

HEART-BURN:

Every morning drink the juice of 2 *turunges* (wild oranges). If not available, then grapefruit juice.

HEMORRHOIDS:

Chew 10-12 juniper-berries first thing in the morning without having eaten or drunk anything else. Then drink a glass of water.

If you don't have any teeth, then crush berries before taking. Repeat for 15 days.

HERPES:

Drink every morning for 10 days a glass of *turunge* (wild orange) or grapefruit-juice.

HIGH BLOOD PRESSURE:

(White cells in the old blood die all the time. The kidney cleans this. Sometimes when going into the veins, the blood clots.)

Have your shoulders and head cupped 2 times a year, preferably in spring and in autumn when it is not too hot or too cold.

WEAK IMMUNE SYSTEM:

Eat 21 raisins with seeds every morning and plenty of almonds.

INSOMNIA:

Never sleep between noon and sunset! Don't drink coffee or tea after sunset!

Any time after sunset when you feel sleepy go to sleep at once. Respect your sleepiness, don't fight it. After 40 days of taking these precautions your sleeping problem will be solved, *Insha Allah.*

ISCHIATITIS:

Heat salt and make 10 minutes massage. Then 10 minutes massage with olive-oil. Tie upper part of the body tightly with wool. Once daily before sleeping.

KIDNEY-STONES:

Take a whole thyme-plant with the roots. Remove the leaves, wash it. Put it into a boiling pot of water and take it off the fire. Leave the plant inside for one day. On the second day drink one glassful in the morning, at noon and in the evening.

Continue treatment until the kidney feels at rest.

LIVER+GALL STONES:

Take a raw egg complete with shell. Wash it, put it in a cup filled with pure lemon juice and cover the cup. Leave overnight. In the morning the hard shell will be melted.

Take the egg with the thin remaining skin carefully out of the cup and use it elsewhere.

Drink the mixture of lemon juice and melted egg skin one or two days in a row without eating anything else.

LOW BLOOD PRESSURE:

Before eating or drinking anything else take 21 raisins in the morning. Better are raisins with seeds. 40 days.

MALARIA:

Take a big spoon of fluid quinine every day and cover the head with a cloth drenched in vinegar.

MASSAGE:

When giving body-massages, heat crystal salt first, wrap into a piece of material and give the massage with it.

MEASLES:

Three times daily eat a big spoon of carob syrup. If not available, then apple-syrup. Best to only eat this during the illness.

MENISCUS:

Give massage of knee every morning and evening with a mixture of olive-oil and petroleum. Then cover with unwashed wool. 7 days.

MORBUS CHRON/CHOLITIS ULCEROSA CHRON:

Roast, crush and mix 20-25 acorns and mix with one glass of honey. Take one table-spoonful every morning before eating or drinking anything else.

1 hour later, mix stinging nettles (cooked like spinach) with cooked wheat, white beans and corn. Add sugar or salt, as you like.

Take a big spoon of olive-oil one hour before lunch.

For 7 days don't eat any meat, no butter, only vegetarian oil, best olive-oil. Better to eat only dry things.

MOUTH INFECTION VIRUS:

Fry 2 tea spoons of black seeds (*Nigella Sativa*). Then smash them and leave them in the mouth for 10-15 minutes. Repeat many times a day.

MUSCULAR DYSTROPHY:

Make a soup out of marrow and eat of it every morning, noon and evening. Eat as many raisins as possible.

Crush and fry black seeds (*Nigella Sativa*) and mix with natural honey and take a spoonful every morning, noon and evening.

Pay *sadaqa*.

MUMPS:

Eat a big spoon of carob syrup every morning, noon and evening. Rub the infected area several times a day with olive-oil.

NAIL-BITING:

Put fingertips in hot pepper.

NEURODERMITIS:

Drink a tablespoon of non-refined olive-oil every morning.

Take a bath every day. Afterwards rub your whole body first with lemon and then with olive oil. Continue treatment until illness disappears.

NOSE-BLEEDING:

Take the hard skin of almonds, roast in oven and crush to fine powder. Sniff!

OVERWEIGHT:

Every morning before eating or drinking anything else eat a salad with plenty of vinegar. One hour later eat and be careful not to mix carbohydrates with proteins.

Best is just to eat of one kind.

During the rest of the day, eat what you want. Continue this diet for 40 days.

PARALYSIS:

Pay *sadaqa.*

Give 3 times daily-morning, noon and evening a massage of 10-20 minutes with olive-oil.

Crush black seeds (*Nigella Sativa*) and boil with water. Then mix with honey and drink as tea in the morning, noon and evening.

PARODONTOSE:

(teeth growing longer, severe gum-infection)

Brush your gum several times a day with a *miswak* until it bleeds. Continue this treatment for three days.

PELVIS-PAIN:

Heat olive-oil and massage.

PIMPLES:

Often a sign of maturity and urgency of getting married.

Give massage of 5 minutes with olive-oil and leave overnight. Or put a leech on each pimple and leave until sucked full when it will fall off by itself.

PREGNANCY & ULTRASOUND:

When a woman is pregnant, it is not even advisable for her to go to a doctor. No-one's had should reach the fetus. It is so wrong and it is against the Divine Rules. When Allah Almighty begins to create and to complete the fetus, angels are working on it. They never want doctors to look at what is inside. They want it to be left as a trust. So don't go. It is the most wrong thing to do to go to doctors every month.

Nowadays most doctors are business-men and make everything as a business. No need for that! When it is clear that a woman is pregnant, don't touch her there, don't go every month to a control.

In the old days we never had a control. No one! Only when the pains of birth came, we called a mid-wife who then said, *"Bismillahi 'r-Rahmani 'r-Rahim.* Oh, my Lord, let your servant come!?" That was all.

I am against every control that the doctors are doing, and the ultra-sound is the most dangerous thing to do for the fetus. It cannot be accepted that the fetus does not get disturbed. No-one should disturb the fetus in its place. No! Therefore the children born, on whose fetus ultrasound was used, very often have some defects: the ultrasound that went through the eyes can make them blind, or through the ears make them deaf, or through the voice make them dumb?

Altogether ultrasound is useless. Even for cancer. The doctors do not know how to find a medicine to cure cancer, so they are doing the ultra-sound for nothing. It is only good for them so that they can take more money. It is not a cure.

Therefore, I am against ultrasound in general.

PSORIASIS:

Rub your skin two times daily first with lemon and then with olive-oil.

RHEUMATISM:

Mix the excrement of bees with yoghurt-whey until it is creamy. Then rub onto rheumatic place and cover with pure wool.

RUNNING NOSE:

Boil eucalyptus leaves in water and inhale several times a day.

SHOCK:

Drink hot milk.

SCHIZOPHRENICS:

Should always wear a *tawiz* and someone powerful should recite prayers (*suras* out of the Holy Quran) for 40 days.

SCORPION-BITE:

Put salt and saliva on the bite.

SEA-SICKNESS:

Don't eat!

Lie down.

Sniff an onion.

SHORT-SIGHTEDNESS:

Every morning before eating or drinking anything else:

Eat 3 crushed cloves of garlic mixed with a spoon of honey. Repeat for 40 days.

SKIN-CANCER:

Rub skin with cotton drenched in vinegar until it turns red. Particularly at night before sleeping. Leave overnight.

Try to go as little as possible into the sun. If it should be necessary, then cover your skin completely. Take special care of also covering your face.

SMOKER'S LEG:

Every morning before eating or drinking anything else drink a full cup of crushed union juice. Repeat until it feels better.

Mix olive-oil and paraffin and give the part of the leg a strong massage for about 15 min.

Eat every morning, noon and evening a salad with apple or grape, vinegar and oil.

SNAKE-BITE:

Suck it out and tie something firmly around it. Then put lemon or vinegar on top or put it in salty water until the pain goes.

SORE THROAT/BEGINNING OF A COLD:

Every morning, noon and evening:

Take some hot water, squeeze lemon juice inside and gargle.

Drink several times a day: boiling water where you first squeeze in some lemon juice then also add the lemon skin and some honey.

SPRAINED ANKLE:

Chop an onion and place the small pieces on the sprained area.

Tie a piece of material around it firmly and leave it there for several hours. In severe cases repeat many times until the swelling is gone.

STAMMERING:

Take the eggshell of a swallow and use as a cup. Drink water in it several times a day, saying, *"Bismillahi 'r-Rahmani 'r-Rahim"* every time.

STERILITY/INFERTILITY:

Take 4 kg of dates and put them in a pot. Put twice as much water and let this boil until half is boiled off. Wait until cooled down.

Squeeze through a piece of cloth and add to this juice 0.33 liters of carob-juice. Keep in fridge.

Drink one Turkish tea glass full every morning and evening.

STOMACH PAIN:

Drink peppermint-tea. If hungry, then drink the water of boiled rice. Or/and:

Roast black seeds (*Nigelle Sativa*) without any oil, then mix with honey. Or:

Take a big spoon of olive-oil and drink.

SUNSTROKE:

Wash head and body with cold water.

GNASHING AND BITING OF TEETH:

(especially during sleep) Bite on a carob!

TORN MUSCLE:

For 4 days move the joint as little as possible. Give a strong massage with olive-oil 3 times a day, each massage for 10- 15 minutes. Wrap the joint with an elastic bandage.

STIFFNESS OF FINGERS WHEN WAKING UP:

This is a sign of weak nerves, so:

Every morning before eating or drinking anything else, eat 21 raisins (preferably with seeds). In the night before going to sleep rub your fingers in olive oil.

VARICOSE VEINS:

Don't cut them, don't have an operation done!

Give a strong massage with olive-oil on them and the area surrounding for 10-15 minutes. Repeat every night for 40 nights.

Pay *sadaqa.*

VAGINAL PARASITE:

1 spoon honey mixed with 1 spoon melted butter.

Eat while still hot every morning before drinking or eating anything else. 40 days.

WATER IN THE LEGS:

Put a leech on outer and inner ankle and leave them there until they fall off by themselves.

WARTS:

Have someone spiritually powerful recite on them. Pay *sadaqa*.

WEAK MEMORY:

Eat 21 raisins with seeds every morning and say *"Bismillahi 'r-Rahmani 'r-Rahim!"* with each one.

YELLOW FEVER:

Squeeze lemons and mix with honey. Drink as a cold drink every morning, noon and evening as much as possible. Pay *sadaqa!*

Eat rice with lemon.

Cover head and stomach with clothes drenched in vinegar.

GLOSSARY:

Bismillahi 'r-Rahmani 'r-Rahim (Arabic):

In the name of Allah, the All-Merciful, the Compassionate. The formula with which every deed should start.

Miswak:

A 4-6 inch long piece of wood, often a twig of the Arak tree, or liquorice-root which is used to clean teeth.

Sadaqa:

Charity, either as a donation or as a good deed.

Tawiz:

A blessed amulet consisting of the 99 Holy Names of Allah, serving as a Protection.

Turkish teaglass/Turkish coffee cup:

0.3 cups, 0.775 pints, 60 cl.

The End

CPSIA information can be obtained
at www.ICGtesting.com
Printed in the USA
BVHW091543291221
625052BV00023B/1471